S0-EFV-118

WITHDRAWN

‖ THE WORLD OF MUSIC ‖
Rock 'n' Roll Music

Published by Creative Education
P.O. Box 227
Mankato, Minnesota 56002
Creative Education is an imprint of The Creative Company.

DESIGN AND PRODUCTION BY ZENO DESIGN

PHOTOGRAPHS BY Corbis (Bettmann; Mitchell Gerber; Hulton-Deutsch
Collection; Lucia; Denis O'Regan; Neal Preston), Getty Images (Aaron
Graubart; Sandra Mu; Charles Trainor/Time & Life Pictures)

Copyright © 2008 Creative Education.
International copyright reserved in all countries.
No part of this book may be reproduced in any form
without written permission from the publisher.
Printed in the United States of America

LIBRARY OF CONGRESS CATALOGING-IN-PUBLICATION DATA

Riggs, Kate.
Rock 'n' roll music / by Kate Riggs.
p. cm. — (World of music)
Includes index.
ISBN 978-1-58341-569-6
1. Rock (Music)—History and criticism—Juvenile literature. I. Title.

ML3534.R543 2008
781.66—dc22   2006102986

First edition

9 8 7 6 5 4 3 2 1

Rock 'n' Roll

YOLO COUNTY LIBRARY
226 BUCKEYE STREET
WOODLAND, CA 95695

MUSIC

KATE RIGGS

CREATIVE EDUCATION

Rock and roll music is a fun kind of music. It started more than 50 years ago. It uses fast beats. It is exciting to listen to. People can sing along to it. They can dance to it, too!

Rock and roll uses rhythms (RI-thumz) *from lots of old African songs.*

Young people loved rock and roll

People think rock and roll started in the 1950s. Lots of young people wanted a different kind of music then. They did not want to listen to the music their parents liked.

Early rock singer Eddie Cochran

Elvis Presley was a famous rock and roll singer. People loved the way he danced around when he sang. He was fun to watch.

Chuck Berry was a great rock and roll guitar player. He wrote songs, too.

Elvis Presley was a popular singer

The Beatles were popular rock and roll singers. They played instruments called guitars in their songs. They used drums to keep the beat, too. People went crazy over the Beatles!

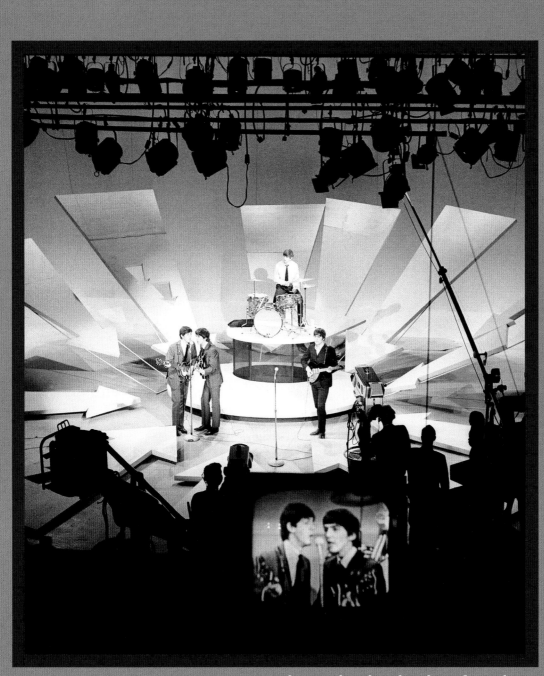

The Beatles played on lots of TV shows

Another group called the Rolling Stones has made music for a long time. Lots of people liked their songs. Some songs sounded mad. Other songs sounded sad.

The Rolling Stones have been playing rock and roll for almost 50 years!

Mick Jagger sang for the Rolling Stones

A kind of music called folk music helped change rock and roll. Folk singers sang about everyday life. They sang about happy times. They sang about bad times, too.

People called hippies really liked the new sounds in folk-rock music.

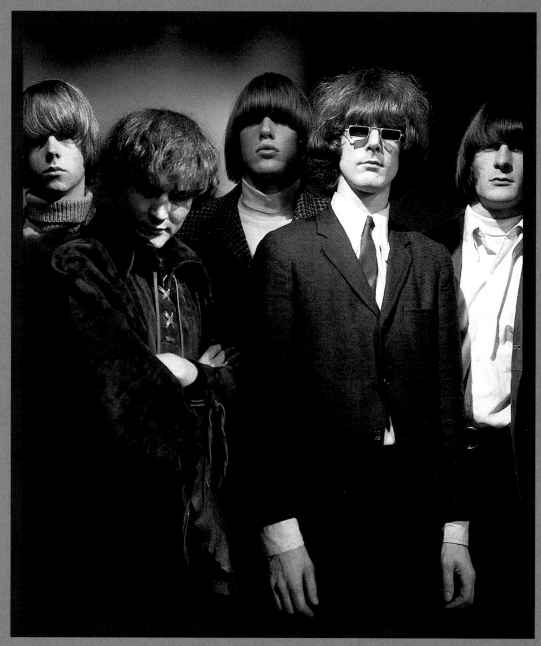

The Byrds played folk-rock music

Other rock and roll singers made new sounds. They started playing electric guitars. They used more drum sounds. Some people thought rock and roll music was too loud!

Jimi Hendrix was a great guitar player

A band called Led Zeppelin played loud rock and roll music. It was called heavy metal. Other groups tried out new sounds, too. Some rap music uses lots of fast talking instead of singing. Some rap songs go so fast that people cannot keep up with the words!

Some rap songs sound very angry. They have hard, fast beats.

Some rock singers have colorful hair

Rock and roll keeps changing today. But bands like U2 still play rock and roll music. They sing songs about what is going on in the world. Lots of people like rock and roll. Young or old, anyone can enjoy rock and roll!

Pop music is a new kind of rock and roll. Lots of young kids like pop music.

Bono (right) sings in the band U2

GLOSSARY

band a group of singers and people who play instruments

electric something that needs to be plugged in to work

folk-rock a mix of folk and rock music

instruments things people play to make music

rhythms patterns of beats found in music

Many rock singers wear flashy clothes

INDEX